Hungary And The War

Darling And Son Publisher

In the interest of creating a more extensive selection of rare historical book reprints, we have chosen to reproduce this title even though it may possibly have occasional imperfections such as missing and blurred pages, missing text, poor pictures, markings, dark backgrounds and other reproduction issues beyond our control. Because this work is culturally important, we have made it available as a part of our commitment to protecting, preserving and promoting the world's literature. Thank you for your understanding.

HUNGARY AND THE WAR

Reprinted from "The Times" by kind permisson of the Editor and Proprietors.

LONDON:
DARLING & SON, LIMITED.

1915.

The articles and the map contained in this pamphlet have been reproduced from *The Times* by the kind permission of the editor and proprietors, to whom this acknowledgment and best thanks are due. The articles, which appeared during January and February 1915, possess more than a passing interest. They have been written by men intimately acquainted with the political life of Hungary, at the critical period of this war, when the change in the person of the Austro-Hungarian Foreign Secretary definitely and openly brought the diplomacy of the Dual Monarchy under the directing will of the Hungarian Premier, Count Stephen Tisza.

HUNGARY AND THE WAR.

I.

A TYRANT OLIGARCHY.

(By a former Correspondent of "The Times" in Austria-Hungary.)

The substitution of Baron de Burian for Count Berchtold as Austro-Hungarian Minister of the Imperial and Royal Household and for Foreign Affairs is the first tangible sign that the stress of war is making itself felt in the Hapsburg dominions. Count Berchtold is not a statesman of marked ability. Indeed, the Emperor Francis Joseph has usually preferred mediocre Ministers. They have been selected as instruments of dynastic policy, and have been sacrificed whenever their usefulness seemed to have ceased. Only when events have been too strong for him has he accepted men whom he might not have chosen of his own free will. Thus he took Beust, a Saxon diplomatist, after the disaster of Sadowa, in 1866, because Beust, as an opponent of Bismarck, advocated the policy of revenge upon Prussia, which was then in favour at the Court of Vienna. Though Beust knew little of Austrian, and still less of Hungarian, affairs, he was entrusted with the delicate work of negotiating, with Deák and Andrássy, the Act of Settlement between Austria and Hungary which has formed the basis of the peculiar arrangement known as the Dual System. It was a one-sided compact which gave Hungary, or rather the oligarchy of Magyar gentry in Hungary, two-thirds of the power in the Monarchy, while leaving Austria to bear two-thirds of the cost. This was done in the vain hope that the Magyars would then lend Austria their support against Prussia.

In return for this hypothetical support, the Dual Settlement left the Magyar oligarchy a free hand to deal as they wished with the Serbo-Croatians, Rumanes, Ruthenes, Swabians, Saxons, Slovaks, and Slovenes, who form the larger, non-Magyar, half of Hungary. Austria divested herself of all power to intervene on their behalf. In later years, even the Archduke Francis Ferdinand found himself unable to mitigate the oppression of the Transylvanian Rumanes by the Magyar authorities. At one moment, indeed, the Emperor Francis Joseph awoke to the true nature of the arrangement he had short-sightedly sanctioned in 1867. As soon as the German victory at Sedan, in September, 1870, had destroyed the Austrian dream of revenge for Sadowa, he attempted to substitute a Federal for the Dual System and to secure elbow-room for the dynasty by reviving the State rights and autonomy of the Slav kingdom of Bohemia. Andrássy, then Hungarian Premier, at once joined hands with Beust and with Bismarck to defeat his project and to compel him to dismiss its putative parent, Hohenwart. Francis Joseph took his revenge by dismissing Beust, but accepted as his successor Andrássy, who strengthened Magyar influence over Austria, and ultimately gave shape to the Austro-German-Magyar *Drang nach Osten* by securing the occupation of Bosnia-Herzegovina in 1878, and by concluding the Austro-German Alliance of 1879.

Austria-Hungary thus became a link in the chain of German influence that was presently to extend from the North Sea to the Aegean and beyond. From time to time Magyar politicians extorted concessions from Austria by toying with the idea of national independence, but in practice all influential Magyar politicians lent themselves to the Austro-German policy of expansion. In this respect there has been no perceptible difference between supporters of Dualism like Tisza, Wekerle, and Khuen-Hedervary, and ostensible apostles of national independence like Apponyi, Kossuth, and the younger Andrássy. They have all recognised that the fate of a Hungary based upon the unconditional rule of the Magyar race over the non-Magyars was bound up with the success of Austro-German plans. They could not, and cannot, break away from Austria without jeopardizing Magyar hegemony. It was the Magyar Nationalist Cabinet under Wekerle, of which Apponyi, Kossuth, and Andrássy were members, that assented, in 1908, to the annexation of Bosnia-Herzegovina; and when, in the summer of 1913, Count Tisza publicly encouraged Bulgaria to assail her allies, Servia and Greece, no dissentient voice was raised in Hungary. The Hungarian Government was cognizant of and helped to prepare the attack upon Serbia which caused the present war. In no part of the Dual Monarchy was the war more popular than among the Magyars. Now that misfortune has overtaken them and they are threatened not only with a Russian but with a Rumanian and eventually with a Serbian invasion, they appear to demand more effectual representation of Magyar interests in the councils of the Crown. Count Berchold was a pseudo-Magyar. Baron de Burian is regarded as a stancher man. But neither his influence nor that of Count Tisza, whose ideas he doubtless represents, is likely to avert the peril that threatens "Magyarland," as the Magyars improperly term Hungary. Like the races which this war of European liberation may free from their yoke, the Magyars will be entitled to just and fair treatment in the re-settlement of Europe; but by their past record and by their abuse of the disproportionate power given them, on a false assumption, in 1867, they have forfeited their claim to rule in future over any race but their own.

The Allied Powers are agreed that the European re-settlement must be inspired by the principle of nationality. It will be but just if Hungary suffers severely from its application, for during the past forty years no European Government has sinned so deeply and persistently against that principle as has her Magyar Government. The old Hungary, whose name and history are surrounded by the glamour of romance, was not the modern "Magyarland." Its boasted constitutional liberties were, indeed, confined to the nobles, and the "Hungarian people" was composed, in the words of Verböczy's Tripartitum Code, of "prelates, barons, and other magnates, also all nobles, but not commoners." But the nobles of all Hungarian races rallied to the Hungarian banner, proud of the title of *civis hungaricus*, John Hunyádi, the national hero, was a Rumane; Zrinyi was a Croat, and many another paladin of Hungarian liberty was a non-Magyar. Latin was the common language of the educated. But with the substitution of Magyar for Latin during the 19th century, and with the growth of what is called the "Magyar State Idea," with its accompaniment of Magyar Chauvinism, all positive recognition of the rights and individuality of non-Magyar races gradually vanished.

The Magyar language itself is incapable of expressing the difference between "Hungarian" and "Magyar." The difference is approximately the same as between "British" and "English." The "Magyar State" set itself to Magyarize education and every feature of public life. Any protest was treated as "incitement against the Magyar State Idea" and was made punishable by two years' imprisonment. It was as though a narrow-minded English Administration should set itself to obliterate all traces of Scottish, Welsh, and Irish national feeling; or as though the Government of India should ignore the existence of all save one race and language in our great Dependency.

In comparison with the Government of "Magyarland," the Government of Austria was a model of tolerance. In Austria, Poles and Ruthenes, Czechs, Germans, Italians, Serbo-Croatians, and Slovenes, were entitled to the public use of their own languages and enjoyed various degrees of provincial self-government. The Austrian side of every Austro-Hungarian banknote bore an indication of its value in every language of the Empire, whereas the Hungarian side was printed in Magyar alone. This was done in order to foster the belief that Hungary was entirely Magyar.

In reality, Hungary is as polygot as Austria. Exact statistics are not obtainable, since the Magyar census returns have long been deliberately falsified for "Magyar State" reasons. Roughly speaking, it may, however, be said that, in Hungary proper, *i.e.*, exclusive of Croatia-Slavonia, where the population is almost entirely Serbo-Croatian, there are perhaps 8,500,000 Magyars, including nearly 1,000,000 professing and a large number of baptized Jews. Against this total there are more than 2,000,000 Germans, including the numerous colonies on the Austrian border, the Swabians of the south and the Saxons of Transylvania; more than 2,000,000 Slovaks, who inhabit chiefly the north-western counties; between three and four million Rumanes, living between the Theiss and the Eastern Carpathians; some 500,000 Ruthenes or Little Russians, who inhabit the north-eastern counties; some 600,000 Serbs and Croats in the central southern counties; 100,000 Slovenes along the borders of Styria and Carinthia; and some 200,000 other non-Magyars, including about 90,000 gipsies, who speak a language of their own. Taking the population of Hungary proper at 18,000,000, the Magyars are thus in a minority, which becomes more marked when Croatia-Slavonia with its population of 2,600,000 Southern Slavs is added.

It would have been possible for the Magyars, after the restoration of the Hungarian Constitution under the Dual Settlement of 1867, to have built up a strong and elastic Transleithan polity based on the recognition of race individualities and equality of political rights for all. The non-Magyars would have accepted Magyar leadership the more readily in that they had been dragooned and oppressed by Austria during the period of reaction after 1849 as ruthlessly as the Magyars themselves. Deák and Eötvös, who were the last prominent Magyar public men with a Hungarian, as distinguished from a narrowly Magyar, conception of the future of their country, pleaded indeed for fair treatment of the non-Magyars, and trusted to the attractive force of the strong Magyar nucleus to settle automatically the question of precedence in the State. But in 1875, when Koloman Tisza, the father of Count Stephen Tisza, took office, these wise counsels were finally and definitely rejected in favour of what Baron Bánffy afterwards defined as "national Chauvinism." Magyarization became the watchword of the State and persecution its means of action. Koloman Tisza concluded with the Monarch a tacit pact under which the Magyar Government was to be left free to deal as it pleased with the non-Magyars as long as it supplied without wincing the recruits and the money required for the Joint Army. The Magyar Parliament became almost exclusively representative of the Magyar minority of the people. Out of the 413 constituencies of Hungary proper, more than 400 were compelled, by pressure, bribery, and gerrymandering, to return Magyar or Jewish Deputies. The Press and the banks fell entirely into Jewish hands, and the Magyarized Jews became the most vociferous of the "national Chauvinists."

Nothing like it has been seen before or since—save after the Turkish Revolution of 1908, when the Young Turks, under Jewish influence, broke away from the relatively tolerant methods of the old regime and adopted the system of forcible "Turkification" that led to the Albanian insurrection of 1910-12, to the formation of the Balkan League, and to the overthrow of Turkey in Europe.

The bitter fruits of the policy of Magyarization are now ripening. The oppressed Rumanes look not towards Austria, as in the old days when their great Bishop Siaguna made them a staunch prop of the Hapsburg dynasty, but across the Carpathians to Bukarest; the Serbo-Croatians of Hungary, Croatia-Slavonia, and Dalmatia, whose economic and political development the Magyars have deliberately hampered, turn their eyes no longer, as in the days of Jellatchich, towards Vienna, but await wistfully the coming of the Serbian liberators; the Ruthenes of the north-east hear the tramp of the Russian armies; the Slovaks of the north-west watch with dull expectancy for the moment when, united with their Slovak kinsmen of Moravia and their cousins, the Czechs of Bohemia, they shall form part of an autonomous Slav province stretching from the Elbe to the Danube. For the Magyars who have thrown to the winds the wisdom of their wisest men, fate may reserve the possession of the fertile and well-watered central Hungarian plain. There they may thrive in modesty and rue at their leisure the folly of having sacrificed their chance of national greatness to the vain pursuit of the "Magyar State Idea" under the demoralizing influence of Austro-German Imperialism.

II.

BUDAPEST IN WAR-TIME.

(BY A NEUTRAL OBSERVER.)

The contrast between Vienna and Budapest is impressive. If Vienna is apathetic, unconcerned, the Hungarian capital is alive with activity and interest. One must visit Budapest in order to get a clear conception of how popular a war can be. No one there will greet you with the words, "We did not want the war. . . . We did not begin the war," which I invariably heard in other cities. On the contrary, they are eager to have you know that this is their war and that they began the conflict. That the conflagration spread over all Europe and has become the greatest war the world has ever known seems to fill every Magyar heart with pride. The exuberance seems to the visitor like a breath of mountain air after the dull atmosphere of Vienna. For the Magyars are proving themselves to be the one strong element in the whole Hapsburg realm.

Hungary, it will be remembered, is practically an independent country, joined for protective and diplomatic purposes by a mutual agreement with the Austrian Empire, under a joint Sovereign. Vienna is nominally the capital and the seat of the Ministry for Foreign Affairs, but every official of importance in that office is a Magyar, including the Minister himself, who takes orders from the head of the Government in Budapest, so that Budapest is now the real capital of the Dual Monarchy.

Crude, ruthless, domineering, the Magyars, who are a minority in their own country, not forming even one-half of the total population of 20 million people, are displaying in the present crisis all the resource, all the strength that they have been storing up for this great event. For to them it is the opportunity they have long looked forward to, of realizing their dreams of Magyar dominion, not merely over the polyglot populations which inhabit the geographically compact Hungary from the Carpathians to the Adriatic, but also over all the Hapsburg countries, and, above all, over Vienna itself. For the Magyar has no patience or tolerance for the Austrians, or for vacillating Austrian methods. In his conversation Austria rarely, if ever, is mentioned.

"We are second only to Germany in moral force." "Germany is our ally." "We feel ourselves in accord with German ideas and ideals." Such phrases as these were repeated to me often, and appear to express accurately the state of mind of the ruling class, though it seems probable that their professed friendship for Germany is based more on policy than on understanding or real sympathy.

The war, as seen through Magyar eyes, is a clear-cut issue. They have one enemy, and only one. No complex problems seem to divert their attention from concentrating their full energy on fighting this enemy—Russia. Russophobia is no vague hypothesis to the Magyars; it is a reality difficult for the foreigner to grasp. Russia is to the Magyars the foster-mother of "Pan-Slavism," not merely in Serbia, but also within the boundaries of Hungary itself. It is the Magyars' firm belief that the existence of the country is being undermined by the tide of "Pan-Slavism," and as this propaganda had been carried on actively in Serbia, the crushing of that country became the immediate concern of Budapest. That the assassination of the Archduke Francis Ferdinand gave the Magyars the opportunity they were looking for is one of the grimmest incongruities in history. I found in Budapest a feeling of the greatest relief that the Archduke, who had been the one obstacle in the way of Magyar domination in the Dual Monarchy, had been removed from the scene.

The rumours that the Magyar leaders were able to convince the Germans that in the Dual Monarchy they alone were vigorous enough to be of efficient service, seems well-founded. I was told by a person who was in a position to know that the decision of the Germans to prosecute vigorously the campaign on the Eastern front was in a large measure influenced by intimations from Budapest, that an advance of the Russians across the Carpathians, would mean the disruption of the Dual Monarchy, and what is more, of the Austro-Hungaro-German Alliance.

Of the war against England or France, only a faint echo reaches Budapest. There is no feeling of enmity against England; on the contrary, the Magyars profess to feel, even at this time, a peculiar bond between themselves and the English. As one man expressed it:—"Our friends the English, who are now our enemies." The Magyars pride themselves on their country life, which they like to believe is closely modelled on the English, and their love of horses, which they feel is another "trait d'union."

The life of the city apparently continues in its usual way. The streets and places of amusement are well filled, though the absence of officers is in striking contrast with Vienna. The Hungarian troops, particularly the "Honvéd" (National Defence) regiments, have acquitted themselves heroically, and the famous Nadasdy Hussars, I have been told, "have covered themselves with glory." I saw a contingent of one of these regiments, and though I was surprised that they apparently have no "field uniform," and wear scarlet breeches and gold lace even in action, I was favourably impressed with their fine soldierly appearance and the excellence of their mounts.

Budapest presents a scene of much military activity. I felt that I was near the war zone, for the possibility of a Russian advance on the city was repeatedly mentioned. The museums have removed their most valuable collections to places of safety, and other defensive measures were being taken.

There is unquestionably a certain uneasiness in the Hungarian capital with regard to Rumania. When I was in the city reports of Rumanian intervention on the side of Russia were being widely circulated, and every Magyar realized the gravity of such an eventuality. Yet I found full confidence among all classes that the Government would be able to handle the situation. A few days later German troops began to pass through Budapest, German officers filled the cafés and hotel corridors. The Magyars breathed more easily. Their confidence in the Government had not been misplaced. The Rumanian crisis passed over.

This implicit faith in the Government rather than in the military authorities is one of the most curious phases of the Hungarian situation. For, in times of peace, party strife and party politics are here more bitter, more unruly, than in any country in Europe. For the time being, outwardly at least, all signs of disagreement have ceased; and during the present war the conduct of affairs has been here alone entrusted wholly to the civil authorities. This is more easily understood when it is realized that, to the Magyars, the Government now in power means not a Cabinet, not a policy, but the personality of one man, the Prime Minister, Count Stephen Tisza.

III.

COUNT TISZA AS DICTATOR.

(BY A NEUTRAL OBSERVER.)

The position which Count Tisza, the Prime Minister of Hungary, occupies in the affairs of the Dual Monarchy is without parallel. He seems to be the one dominant personality who, by his uncompromising attitude, is able to control the turbulent elements within his own country.

Count Tisza is essentially a man of action, who lives in the present—for the present. He is not given to vague speculation nor to consideration of possibilities. Concrete, impersonal, vehement, absolute, he knows of one road, and only one to attain his end. An ardent Calvinist, in a land where the nobility are chiefly Roman Catholics, he is able to reconcile his Calvinism with duelling, steeplechasing, and the ownership of a racing stable. Though a Conservative, believing that "the rule of iron is the rule of God," he is maintained in power by a so-called "Party of Work," which is a pseudonym for the old "Liberal," or Dualist, Party which, with one brief interval has ruled Hungary since 1867. Violently hated by his many political opponents, he remains impassive to their jibes for long periods, and then strikes suddenly with all the strength at his command. He has had them ejected from Parliament and has met and wounded many of them on the duelling-ground. Withal he is a *bon père de famille*, and takes the greatest interest in his vast estates, for he is a member of the landed gentry, rather than of the aristocracy. He inherited his title from an uncle.

From his father, Koloman Tisza, who was for 15 years Prime Minister of Hungary, he inherited the most important feature of his policy, the "Magyarizing" of Hungary. This appears to be Count Tisza's most cherished aim. In its pursuit he has unquestionably discriminated against the non-Magyar population of the Kingdom, but has on the other hand strengthened the position of the Magyars, not only in their own land, but in the affairs of the Dual Monarchy.

It is, I believe, above all the personality of Count Tisza himself that has determined the relatively preponderant position occupied by the Magyars in the councils of the Germano-Austro-Hungarian Alliance. It would seem to bear out the statement that, no great man having appeared on the German horizon, the German Emperor is pleased to deal directly with the Hungarian Prime Minister, in whom he recognizes the qualities of a great statesman.

In endeavouring to estimate the position of Germany and Austria-Hungary after seven months of warfare, it must be borne in mind that almost the entire burden of military responsibility rests with the Germans. On the other hand, Germany looks to Budapest to be able to keep the peace in the Balkans. By playing off Bulgaria against Rumania, by throwing a comparatively large force of German troops on the Rumanian frontier at a critical juncture, and by other similar measures, the Hungarian Prime Minister has, up to the present, been able to do his share. Should attempts be made, at the instance of Germany, to purchase Italian neutrality by territorial concessions at the expense of Austria, it is also expected that the Magyar Government would contrive to secure Austrian assent, on condition that the territorial integrity of Hungary should be inviolate.

From the Magyar point of view the establishment of an independent Kingdom of Poland, including Galicia as a buffer State between Russia and Hungary, seemed, to the persons with whom I spoke, of the utmost importance. This may account, in part, for the attitude of indifference of the Monarchy with regard to the fate of this Austrian province. The crushing of the " Greater Serbia " movement is to be secured, not so much by the conquest of Serbia, as by the removal of Russophil agitators, and particularly by a change in the Serbian dynasty. Among the Magyars, there appeared to be full confidence that, with German aid, this programme will be carried out.

Of Austrian aims I heard no mention. The general impression I gathered was that in the Dual Monarchy, many feel that Austrian ambitions and plans are secondary to those of the two other members of the Alliance. Austria will pay dearly for the war, no matter what the outcome; to lose as little as possible, seems her chief concern.

The situation of Germany herself is more difficult to summarise. Though apparently unimpaired in vigour, yet the burden of carrying on the war, not merely on her own frontiers, but even in the remoter parts of the Dual Monarchy, would seem to be a task greater than was contemplated. The Germans expected that the Austro-Hungarian forces would not only be able to hold their own lines, but also to render efficient assistance elsewhere. There is consequently much criticism of the Austrians, even among the " people " of Germany, and the Austrians are universally considered an added burden.

The idea that the Germans hope to be able to carry the war to a successful conclusion on all frontiers simultaneously was everywhere discounted. Their plan seems to be to crush Russian resistance, or, failing in that, to detach Russia from the Allies by concessions of a sweeping nature. I heard much talk of the growing influence of Germanophil sentiments in certain influential quarters in the Russian capital, and in the event of finding no solution by force of arms, this was to be relied upon. Should German plans on the Eastern front be realised, there is confidence that, by turning full attention to the West, the German forces will be able speedily to break through the French and British lines. I was repeatedly assured that the best German troops and generals have been employed against the Russians. The object of the Western campaign is alleged to be to wear down the resisting power of the Allies, so that with the sudden arrival of new forces a decisive victory may possibly be secured.

While they profess sentiments to the effect that Germany will fight until victory is secured, to many Germans peace even at the present time would not be unwelcome. For they seem to realize that their extended line from Lodz to Lille cannot with safety be advanced in both directions and that they stand to-day at the height of their fortunes. Whether the peace that the Germans speak of will be a lasting peace seems to their leading thinkers a matter difficult to determine.

IV.

COUNT TISZA AND GERMANY.

The writer of this article is a Hungarian publicist of great experience who, after a visit to Hungary, has now returned to a neutral country.

During the past fortnight Austro-Hungarian public attention has been diverted from the battlefields to the change in the Ministry of Foreign Affairs. The reasons for Count Berchtold's supersession by Baron de Burian are being eagerly discussed, if not by the public Press, which fears the blue pencil of the Censor, by politicians and such strata of the public as take a lively interest in what is going on behind the scenes. In Austria-Hungary you get scores of explanations merely for the asking. The advocates of the theory of the "stronger fist" will tell you that Count Berchtold is too much of a *grand seigneur* to cope with the exigencies of the present case. They smile knowingly and tell you that a strong man was wanted to keep Italy and Roumania in order. Others, who feel the German superiority as a slight, will try to convince you that Baron de Burian was the right man to protect Austro-Hungarian interests on the battlefield as well as later on when the Peace Congress will meet.

These arguments are obviously too trite to carry conviction. They will not convince the student of Austro-Hungarian affairs, who is warned by experience not to accept superficial reasons for such an important event as the change of a Foreign Minister has always been with the Emperor and King.

One fact has been strongly accentuated—the intimate relationship between Count Tisza and Baron de Burian. The Hungarian Prime Minister is not famous for possessing many friends. He is a man of many contradictions—austere and impulsive, honest and astute, calculating and rash, Bible-preaching and tyrannical, often violent, but always loyal to his ideas. Surrounded by a host of sycophants, he has scarcely more than half-a-dozen friends. Baron de Burian's psychological portrait would, to the superficial observer, appear like a replica of Count Tisza's features.

This is not so. Baron de Burian has the energy of a hard-working man. He is of indefatigable industry, but his mind is not fertile. He lacks the power of great conceptions. But none is more persevering, none surer of success than he, if bent upon carrying out a given scheme. Fascinated by Count Tisza's doubtless very interesting individuality and convinced that his friend is the very greatest statesman of our age, Baron de Burian is unconditionally devoted to the Hungarian Prime Minister. His highest ambition is to be the trusted collaborator of his friend. The Foreign Minister will never dream of becoming more than the confidential manager of Count Tisza's affairs. Baron de Burian is proud of being the trustee of his friend's legacy. And legacy it is, for it is an open secret that the palace at the Ballplatz([1]) might have been Count Tisza's for the asking. He preferred to give it in trust and to keep to his business in Hungary.

Why? Is Count Tisza of opinion that he can do more important work in Budapest than in Vienna? And, if so, what is his work there? Parliament is practically non-existent, domestic policy is subordinated to the military administration, and the home affairs of Hungary disappear behind the war façade of the Dual Monarchy. Let me, at this point, remind you of Count Tisza's recent visit to the Kaiser. He saw the German Emperor not as the representative of Hungary, for Hungary has no title to individual representation abroad. The Hungarian Prime Minister could not have represented the Emperor and King, whose constitutional representative is the Minister of the Imperial and Royal Household—a dignity always vested in the Minister for Foreign Affairs. In undertaking a mission abroad the Hungarian Prime Minister discarded Count Berchtold, and in doing so he infringed the Fundamental Law of 1867, which regulates the respective positions of Austria and Hungary within the framework of the Dual Monarchy.

Nevertheless, I have good reason to believe that Count Tisza does not consider his act as a breach of the Constitution, but as "an evolution of the arrangement of 1867." This is an important fact which gives more than a mere clue to the dismissal (for such it was) of Count Berchtold. It sheds a brilliant light upon the present condition of the Austro-Hungarian Monarchy and upon the policy which Count Tisza is bent upon following.

Imagine, for one moment, Austria-Hungary as separated from Germany. What idea does the Dual Monarchy represent? Historically destined to serve as a buffer between two powerful and antagonistic racial currents (Slav and Teuton), its obvious task was to realise the principle of nationality by way of federation. Broad-minded politicians in both halves of the Monarchy

---

([1]) The Austro-Hungarian Foreign Office.

have never tired of propagating this idea as the only means of filling the geographical conception known as "Austria-Hungary" with the contents of real life. The Monarchy is like a body of many arteries, but lacking a heart to regulate the circulation of the blood. It is limp and lifeless. Till 1870 the doctors experimented and tried to infuse the arteries with German blood. No heart responded. After a brief attempt at recognizing the importance of the Slav element, political life relapsed into petty intrigues between the Governments of the two halves of the Monarchy—a mere struggle for ascendancy. The Monarch was moved by his sympathy for Austria and by fear of a possible rising in Hungary. To reconcile Budapest he left the Hungarian Government a free hand with regard to domestic policy. The logical consequence was the stern accentuation by the Hungarian Governments of Magyar ascendancy in Hungary, and, in order to counteract the complaints of the non-Magyars, utter subservience to the foreign policy of the Hapsburgs. Hence the consent of the Wekerle Government to the annexation of Bosnia-Herzegovina and its complicity in Aehrenthal's various adventurous schemes.

Count Tisza, who is a very pronounced individuality, could not be expected to follow the trodden path. He was looking out for new departures. A thought that ever haunted him was the part his father played during the Balkan crisis in the seventies of last century. At that time Koloman Tisza was the mouthpiece of the Monarchy. Every declaration of international importance was made in the Hungarian Parliament. At that time Hungary was the leading partner of the Monarchy; the Foreign Minister (Andrássy) was a Hungarian. Now it may seem that Count Tisza was merely following the example of his father and, by housing Baron de Burian at the Ballplatz, creating a similar position. This explanation must be discarded. Count Andrássy was not the manager of Koloman Tisza's affairs and never allowed him so much as a counselling voice in the international business of the Monarchy. Koloman Tisza was merely the mouthpiece of Andrássy. The position, at present, is the reverse. The change, however, goes far beyond the mere personal aspect. Count Andrássy valued the alliance with Germany as an insurance against Russia. His policy was limited to the economic penetration of the Balkans, and though he might have cherished the idea of an ultimate annexation of Bosnia-Herzegovina, he strongly repudiated the advisability of further territorial acquisitions in the Near East.

Count Tisza's political conception is entirely different. To him the alliance with Germany means much more than a mere insurance. It means unconditional collaboration towards territorial expansion. He is the Hungarian representative of the *Drang nach Osten*. The concordance of his policy with that of the German Foreign Office, combined with the fact that Austria can, at present, boast of no statesman gifted with ability, or even with energy, has made Tisza the man of the hour. As Burian is the Hungarian Prime Minister's trustee at the Ballplatz, so is Tisza the Statthalter of Germany in Austria-Hungary.

Now there is still a problem to be solved. It is not likely that a statesman of Count Tisza's self-conscious individuality should easily submit to being the mere tool of another will-power. He has ambitions of his own and these are Magyar ambitions. Hitherto, there could be distinguished two different tendencies in Magyar political thought. The one has been bent upon Magyarizing Hungary within the Dual Monarchy, the other professed to aim at Magyarizing an independent Hungary. Tisza, who has never believed in the theory of independence, nevertheless succeeded in satisfying its adherents at the outbreak of the war. It is a fact that has given vent to much speculation, that the Hungarian Independence Party made no use of the present opportunity to try and attain its political ideal. There seemed, as far back as last August, a tendency at work to start a rising in Hungary, but the very leaders of the Independence Party put an early stop to it.

I am told on unquestionable authority that the conversion of the Independence Party was brought about in a conference in which Count Tisza expounded his political conception of "Magyar Imperialism." The name as such is not a new one. It has been exploited by a Budapest paper, the *Budapesti Hirlap* for many years past. Originally it was to mean the complete Magyarization of Hungary. Count Tisza has given it a new sense. Its aim is the ascendency of Hungary within the Monarchy, the political centre of which is to be transferred to Budapest. This is what the Hungarian Prime Minister understood by coining the new phrase, "Evolution of the arrangement of 1867." He convinced the leaders of the Independence Party that what he proposed to realize was much more valuable than independence, and Count Apponyi, M. Justh, and Count Andrássy have become the most fervent partisans of intimacy with Germany. The allusion in Count Tisza's New Year's speech to the "centralists" in Austria and to Hungary's present position in the Monarchy will be more clearly understood in the light of this explanation, though it is not to be wondered at that its meaning has been somewhat dark to the Viennese politicians. Again, it will be understood why Count Tisza preferred to stay on in Budapest instead of taking up his residence in Vienna, where Baron de Burian will not only transact the foreign business, but will be ready to promote Count Tisza's scheme in his capacity as a Minister of the Imperial House.

Printed by Libri Plureos GmbH in Hamburg, Germany